Hernan...
A
Gold and Glory

This book is dedicated to
Sandra Anderson,
who got me started on biographies.

Acknowledgments

Many thanks to David Dickel and the Florida Department of State, Division of Historical Resources, Bureau of Archaeological Research for allowing me to view the artifacts from De Soto's winter encampment in Tallahassee. I am grateful to Brian Nolan, who helped me with the pronunciation of Spanish names, and to my son David, who read my manuscript for clarity and readability. I would never have figured out how to pronounce the Native American names and places mentioned in this book without the help of renowned De Soto scholar Charles Hudson, Ph.D., Emeritus Franklin Professor of Anthropology, University of Georgia. I am even more deeply indebted to Dr. Hudson for reading this book in manuscript stage and making suggestions and corrections. If there are any errors, however, they are mine. Finally, I want to thank my husband, Benjamin, whose research enabled me to finish this book much faster.

Picture credits: *American Indian Design & Decoration*, Dover Publications, Inc.: 16, 69. Bruce Dupree: cover, title page, maps (De Soto expedition map is based on a map provided by Dr. Charles Hudson), 14, 31, 40, 70, 71, 75, 88, 92. Benjamin T. Gibbons III (with permission of the Florida Department of State, Division of Historical Resources, Bureau of Archaeological Research): 44. Library of Congress: 52, 82, 97. North Wind Picture Archives: 28, 62.

Words in **bold** in the text of this book are defined in the Glossary on page 106.

Hernando De Soto
A Search for Gold and Glory

Faye Gibbons

Original illustrations
by Bruce Dupree

CRANE HILL
PUBLISHERS

Original illustrations by Bruce Dupree

Developmental and copy editing
by Tanya Martin

Published by Crane Hill Publishers
www.cranehill.com

Printed in the United States of America

Library of Congress Cataloging-in-Publication Data

Gibbons, Faye.
  Hernando De Soto: a search for gold and glory / Faye Gibbons;
original illustrations by Bruce Dupree.
      v. cm.
Includes bibliographical references and index.
Contents: A Spanish conquistador in the New World -- Florida at last! --
Apalachee -- Treasure -- Marching through Coosa -- Facing Tascaluza --
Another battle -- De Soto loses hope.
  ISBN 1-57587-198-X trade paper   ISBN 1-57587-205-6 hardcover
  1. Soto, Hernando de, ca. 1500-1542--Juvenile literature. 2.
Explorers--America--Biography--Juvenile literature. 3.
Explorers--Spain--Biography--Juvenile literature. 4. America--Discovery
and exploration--Spanish--Juvenile literature. 5. Southern
States--Discovery and exploration--Spanish--Juvenile literature. [1. De
Soto, Hernando, ca. 1500-1542. 2. Explorers. 3. America--Discovery and
exploration--Spanish.] I. Dupree, Bruce, ill. II. Title.
  E125.S7 G53 2002
  970.1'6'092--dc21

                              2002000587

10   9   8   7   6   5   4   3   2   1

Contents

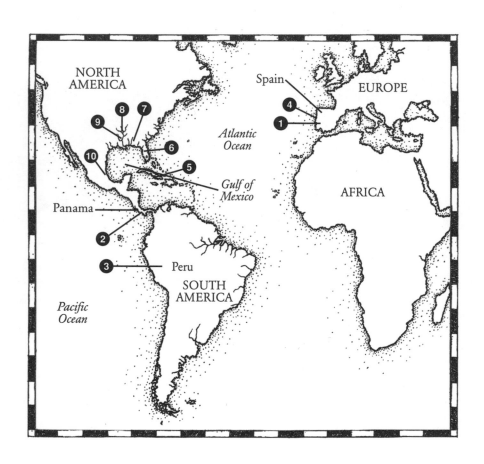

NORTH
AMERICA

Spain

EUROPE

⑧ ⑦

⑨

Atlantic
Ocean

④
①

⑥

⑩

⑤

Gulf of
Mexico

AFRICA

Panama

②

③ — Peru

SOUTH
AMERICA

Pacific
Ocean

Time Line

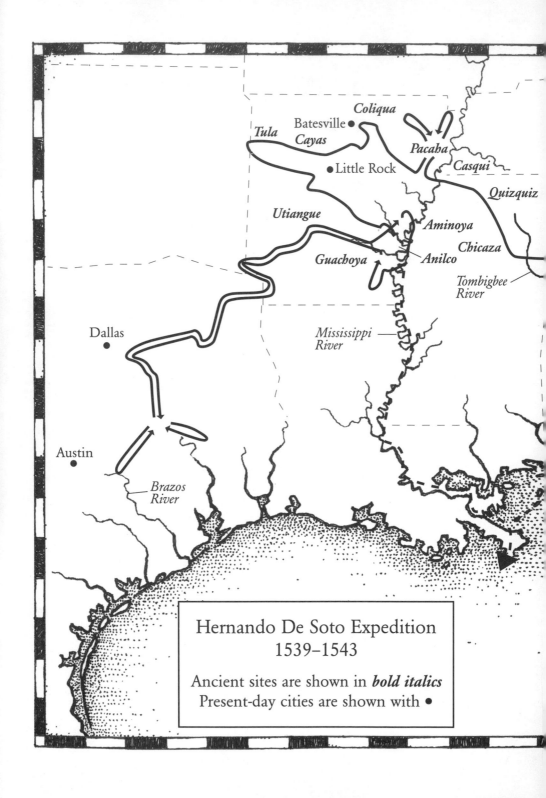

Coliqua

Batesville ●

Tula

Cayas

● Little Rock

Pacaha

Casqui

Quizquiz

Utiangue

Aminoya

Guachoya

Anilco

Chicaza

Dallas ●

Mississippi River

Tombigbee River

Austin ●

Brazos River

Hernando De Soto Expedition
1539–1543

Ancient sites are shown in **bold italics**
Present-day cities are shown with ●

Chiaha

Coste

Newport

Carters · Coosa
Itaba

Ulibahali
Rome · · Cartersville

Cofitachequi
Camden ·

pafalaya

Moundville

Talisi
· Childersburg
· Sylacauga
Uxapita
· Wetumpka
· Montgomery
Atahachi

Milledgeville ·

Macon ·

Selma ·

Mabila

Piachi
Alabama River

Oglethorpe ·

Achuse

Anhaica
Tallahassee ·

Napituca
Live Oak ·

Pensacola
Bay

Bay of the
Horses

Ocale

Urriparacoxi

Ozita
· Ruskin

Gulf of
Mexico

Tampa Bay

Tracing De Soto's Trail

Hernando De Soto was a Spanish explorer and **conquistador**. He began his adventures as a teenager. At 14, he first set sail. He was part of an **expedition** to Panama in the New World. At 20, he gained the rank of captain. He became known for his bravery, his boldness, and for his skills as a horseman and a soldier. De Soto's final expedition took him from the Gulf Coast of Florida, across the Mississippi River, to the vicinity of present-day Little Rock, Arkansas. He is known as the first European explorer to reach the great river. In 1542, he died on the bank of the Mississippi and was laid to rest in its depths.

It has been more than 450 years since De Soto and his army marched across a new **continent**. But evidence of his journey remains. He is remembered in many Southeastern names—of towns, attractions, shopping centers, and developments. In his time, he was called Soto. Some scholars use this original name, while others refer to him as De Soto. We will do the same.

The exact route the expedition followed from 1539 to 1543 has never been completely clear. Today, many scholars and scientists are working to find the actual De Soto trail. Like detectives looking for clues, they go to written accounts of the expedition. These accounts are known as **chronicles** or journals. Some were written by men who were part of the expedition. Through the chronicles, we can learn which rivers, mountains, forests,

Authors of the De Soto Chronicles

This book is based on three "eyewitness" accounts by members of the expedition and other accounts written by historians.

Rodrigo Rángel was De Soto's secretary. He kept a daily record that included details of time and place.

Luis Hernández de Biedma was the **factor** of the expedition. A factor acts as an agent for another. Biedma represented the king of Spain. He was to make sure that the king received his fair share of any treasure found. His brief chronicle included important compass directions.

An unnamed Gentleman from Elvas, a Portuguese nobleman, was also part of the expedition. His record provided details left out by others.

Garcilaso de la Vega was a historian of Inca Indian and Spanish heritage. He was not part of the expedition, but he talked with survivors. His version is a romantic and not always factual account.

swamps, plains, and native villages the explorers saw. Compass directions are often given, as are the number of days it took to travel from one point to another. Descriptions of the natives and their homes, social customs, and daily life are sometimes included.

De Soto's army followed existing Indian trails. Much later, those trails became roads. Some eventually became highways. Very old maps of early roads hint where the expedition might have traveled. Walking these trails, today's scholar-detectives search for geographic features noted in the chronicles. They time how long it takes to walk from one point to the next. They then compare the time with the written accounts to see if it is a likely route. De Soto's expedition normally traveled twelve to fifteen miles each day, on horseback and on foot.

Archaeologists are part of the search for De Soto's trail. **Archaeology** is the study of people and **civilizations** through evidence left behind—fossils, skeletons, and products of everyday life. When archaeologists find Indian **artifacts** of the right age at the same place as Spanish artifacts of the same age, it can confirm a location as a De Soto site. With each discovery, we develop a better understanding of America's native peoples. We see what our land was like before conquerors and settlers from across the Atlantic changed it forever.

In addition to being known as a bold leader and explorer, Hernando De Soto is known for helping to end the Indian way of life. He was ruthless in his dealings with the natives, as were most Europeans. Indians who did not do as he asked suffered brutal consequences. As we trace his final journey, we learn about the fascinating and varied Native American cultures of the sixteenth century. But sadly, we also learn of the cruel ways of the Spanish conquerors who overcame them in the name of God, gold, and glory.

CHAPTER ONE

A Spanish Conquistador in the New World

Hernando De Soto rode into the court of Atahualpa on a magnificent horse. He wore full armor and a plumed helmet. De Soto was a top officer in Francisco Pizarro's army. He knew he could show no fear in facing the ruler of the vast Inca empire.

It was important for a conquistador to look splendid. A show of bravery was important, too. Although surrounded by a huge Inca army, De Soto took only an **interpreter** and a small group of soldiers with him.

The emperor Atahualpa was seated just outside his palace with nobles, servants, aides, and 400 guards. The Incas had never seen horses before. Most natives were afraid of the large beasts. Yet Atahualpa did not flinch. He refused to look at De Soto or the horse, even when the steed's hot breath stirred the golden fringe on his tasseled crown.

This ruler was a man who had taken a kingdom away from his own brother. He was worshipped, feared, and respected by his subjects. He was called the Child of the Sun. As De Soto and the interpreter spoke, Atahualpa stared at the ground. He would not say a word. He intended to insult the Spaniards. They were intruders in his land.

Conquistadors were not used to being insulted. This was unacceptable! De Soto sprang onto his saddle. His horse reared, turned, and charged down the courtyard. He gave a grand show of horsemanship, complete with leaps and turns. He galloped toward the emperor at full speed, pulling back at the very last moment. The horse halted so quickly and so close to Atahualpa that it snorted foam over the royal robes. Some of the Inca guards pulled back in alarm. Atahualpa was furious. That night, those guards paid for their cowardice with their lives.

De Soto was most likely pleased with his performance. He had shown that a conquistador would not be ignored.

Incan llama crafted in solid gold

Who were the Incas?

The vast empire of the Inca Indians was called the Four Corners of the World. It stretched over what is today Peru, Ecuador, and parts of Columbia and Bolivia. The Incas were an advanced civilization. They built magnificent structures and created beautiful objects of solid gold.

Hernando De Soto was not always so grand. He was born about 1500 in the Spanish province of Extremadura. It was a windy, dry, poor region. Some people raised sheep and attempted to farm the harsh, dusty land. De Soto's father was a **hidalgo**, a gentleman squire, in the village of Jerez de los Caballeros. His family belonged to the lowest level of Spanish nobility. These nobles had rank, but no real wealth. They didn't herd sheep or work the land. That was for peasants or slaves. The only honorable profession for sons of hidalgos was a military career.

The men of Extremadura were renowned as soldiers. Several famous explorers came from the region: Hernando Cortéz, Francisco Coronado, and Vasco Núñez de Balboa, who was De Soto's neighbor. Balboa made history in 1513. He crossed the **isthmus** of Panama and discovered the Pacific Ocean.

Spain became a nation of warriors by fighting the Moors. The Moors were Muslims from North Africa. After centuries of warfare, Spaniards finally drove the enemy from their land in the late 1400s. Life was still hard, however, and there remained much to fear. At night few people ventured outside their crowded, walled towns. Raw sewage ran through ditches along the narrow streets and alleys. Rats, dogs, and pigs spread the filth from those ditches. The sewage smelled terrible and it spread disease.

Unpleasant as it was inside the walls, it was even more dangerous outside. Outlaws roamed the countryside, robbing and killing. There were wolves and bears in the forests. Young men had to become tough at an early age.

Little is known about De Soto's childhood. He must have been hardy. Only the strongest survived droughts, famines, and the plague. Often such disasters killed hundreds of thousands. Perhaps those who lived developed a toughness for enduring disease and near starvation.

Most Spanish people of the time, even nobles like the De Sotos, lived in near poverty. Because they had little else, hidalgos clung to pride and honor. De Soto's village name honors an order of knights. Growing up, the boy heard tales of knights and **chivalry**. He learned of Spaniards who had gone to the New World and become rich. He began to imagine this for himself. It was the only route for an ambitious young man to rise in the world.

Spain's religion supported these ambitions. Part of the purpose in going to the New World was to take Christianity to the natives. But it did not have to be by peaceful means. Europeans believed that native peoples were **heathens**, unbelievers. They were looked down upon because they did not practice the same faith. De Soto was a firm Catholic. The God of sixteenth-century Catholics approved of slaughtering the unbeliever.

Because of his noble birth, De Soto had some schooling. He also trained in the skills of a soldier: horseback riding, sword fighting, and the rules of chivalry. When he was 14, De Soto became a **page**, a knight-in-training. He was assigned to Pedro Arias Davila, known as Don Pedrarias. In 1514, the king sent Pedrarias to Panama (then known as Darién). He was **adelantado**, or governor, of the **colony**. The young De Soto went with Pedrarias and his family. It would be

Now Hear This

Conquistadors were required by the church and the king to read an official statement, the **requerimiento**, to the natives. The Indians, of course, did not understand it. Sometimes they did not even hear it. They often deserted before the invaders reached them. Then, the statement was read to an empty village. The requerimiento demanded that the Indians accept Christianity. They had to agree to be ruled by Spain. "If you do not do this…we will make war in every place and by every means…. We will take you and your wives and children and make them slaves…and will do you all the harm and evil we can…." The Spaniards were true to their word.

more than twenty years before he returned to Spain.

Some believe a romance soon began between the teenage De Soto and Isabel, Pedrarias's daughter. It's possible, and, if that was the case, it might explain much of De Soto's desire for fame and success. Only by raising himself higher could he hope to win permission to marry Isabel.

De Soto was successful beyond his wildest dreams. By 18, as part of Pedrarias's army, he had become a bold and brave soldier. He was often a leader in attacks against the Central American natives. His reward was more responsibility, gold, and Indian slaves. He became known as a man who was not afraid of danger. His skills with horses and weapons were widely known. He didn't mind killing, but he avoided it if he could. Often, he used words to persuade. He usually showed sound judgment. De Soto listened to the opinions of those under him before making big decisions. He was a strong leader, and his men looked up to him.

For these reasons, Francisco Pizarro made De Soto his first lieutenant. This was why Pizarro chose De Soto for that first meeting with Atahualpa.

De Soto's tricks on horseback had been meant to impress the emperor. But his efforts did not work.

Shortly afterward, Pizarro organized an attack on the Incas and took Atahualpa prisoner. The emperor bargained with Pizarro for his life. He agreed to pay a **ransom** to gain his freedom.

A large room, more than 20 feet long by 17 feet wide, was to be filled with gold and silver. Atahualpa's subjects brought many valuable, beautiful objects from all over the kingdom. There were cups, bowls, pitchers, plates, jewelry, knives, masks, and decorative and ceremonial objects. Many were made of gold and precious gems. The Spaniards did not view these objects as art. They didn't care about their beauty or craftsmanship. Nor did they care what symbolic meaning they had to the Incas. They simply wanted gold, lots of it. They melted down most of the gold into bars so they could transport it more easily.

It had taken the Incas about eight months to gather the gold and silver. The task done, Atahualpa demanded that he be released. He had given the Spanish what they wanted. But Pizarro had other plans. He couldn't risk Atahualpa's thousands of warriors taking revenge on his small force of fewer than 200. He sent De Soto away on an errand and put Atahualpa on trial for some made-up charges. Then, in the middle of the night in August 1533, he had him strangled. De Soto was displeased with Pizarro's actions, but it was too late to do anything about it when he returned.

Despite his feelings about Atahualpa's death, De Soto accepted a large share of the gold. He was suddenly a wealthy man. When he returned to Spain in 1536, he was so rich that he loaned money to the king.

The German artist Albrecht Dürer saw some of the New World treasure that was brought back to the court of King Charles. He wrote:

> *I saw the things which have been brought to the King from the new land of gold.... All the days of my life I have seen nothing that rejoiced my heart so much as these things, for I saw among them wonderful works of art, and I marveled.... Indeed, I cannot express all that I thought there.*

For two years, De Soto fought in various battles in Peru. He was eventually named governor of Cuzco, the fabled Inca capital deep in the Andes mountains. He finally sailed home to Spain, a hero.

Upon his return, De Soto made his home in the city of Seville. He purchased a large house, hired servants, and bought expensive clothing. He did not forget his family. He was generous with money and favors. He surrounded himself with fellow soldiers also back from Peru. The adventurers probably told and retold their stories of the New World. Their feats grew bolder and more remarkable with each telling.

De Soto's thoughts turned to marriage. He was now in a position to choose a wife from an important family. Perhaps he followed his heart as well, for he proposed to Isabel de Bobadilla. Like other brides from wealthy families, she brought with her a good **dowry** to add to her husband's fortune. She was also a good match because her experiences were similar to De Soto's. As the daughter of Pedrarius, Isabel had lived in the New World most of her life.

De Soto was rich and famous. He had married the woman of his dreams. He lived in a beautiful home. His life was enviable, yet he was not content. Money, jewels, servants, and even remembered victories grew stale. He missed his adventurous life in the New World. And he still had the fever for gold. De Soto was sure there was more treasure to be found.

The desire for power probably drew him, too. In the New World, he might claim an empire—titles and land that could be passed on to his children. He could be both rich and powerful, with many slaves.

So he traveled to see Charles I, King of Spain. A deal was made. The king gave De Soto the right to conquer and govern **La Florida.** This name refers to an area much larger than the present-day state. La Florida was the entire region that later became the southeastern United States.

The agreement with the king allowed De Soto to keep four-fifths of any riches he found. In return, De Soto would pay all the expenses of the expedition. He was to start a settlement in the new colony and build forts and harbors. The king named him governor of Cuba and adelantado—military governor—of Florida. De Soto would first go to Cuba and set up operations there. He was then free to begin his grand adventure.

Neither De Soto nor King Charles seemed to give much thought to the earlier Florida expeditions. Those had been dismal failures. Nothing had been gained. The majority who made those journeys died. De Soto refused to be dismayed. His experience would be different. He had counted on good fortune all his life. So far, he had accomplished all he set out to achieve.

News of De Soto's expedition spread far and wide. Men from all over Spain, Portugal, and other parts of Europe rushed to volunteer. The chance to get rich was too tempting to resist.

A good number of those he selected for the journey were fellow soldiers from Peru. Some were relatives. Several were teenagers, some were blacks, and six were

Florida or Bust

De Soto was not the first explorer to reach Florida. Juan Ponce de León discovered and named the land La Florida in 1513. His colony failed in 1521.

In 1526, Lucas Vásquez de Ayllón explored the coast of Florida. His colony also failed. Most of the colonists died of illness or starvation.

In 1528, Pánfilo de Narváez searched for gold in Florida. He had many battles with the Indians. He and his men finally reached the Gulf of Mexico. They built boats to attempt an escape. Most of them perished.

women. One was eventually revealed as a woman disguised as a man! Many were prepared to invest their own money in the venture. No one would get a salary, but if they found riches, each would get a share. Those who invested would receive more, in proportion to their investment.

Because he planned to start a colony, De Soto also included a number of skilled craftsmen: tailors, shoemakers, carpenters, and ironsmiths, among others. The soldiers may have looked down on these ordinary workers. But before the journey's end, they would come to realize the value of these men.

De Soto sailed from Spain toward Cuba in the spring of 1538. His party included about eleven vessels. Sources don't agree on the exact number. His secretary, Rodrigo Rángel, wrote that there were nine ships, two

caravels (light sailing ships), and two **brigantines** (light sailing ships that can also be rowed). Historians don't agree on the exact number of people, either. There were definitely more than 600, possibly as many as 100 more. In addition, there were servants, slaves, and camp followers.

De Soto's personal helpers included nearly 100 guards, pages, secretaries, servants, stable hands, and a chamberlain (a servant to run his household). The horses numbered more than 300. He took several dozen for his own use. De Soto almost certainly chose a sturdy Spanish breed. These horses were small but fast. They could haul heavy loads for long distances, yet ate less than larger horses. De Soto knew that the Indians in Florida did not have horses. On horseback, his men would have the advantage in any fight. He counted on the natives being afraid of the horses.

De Soto took dogs, too. These were not pets. They were greyhounds, vicious war dogs. These animals were trained to kill on command. They wore spiked collars to prevent anyone from choking them. They could be used to capture runaway slaves or to punish Indians who displeased their masters.

De Soto's wife Isabel accompanied him to the New World. While De Soto set off to Florida, Isabel would govern Cuba in his place. It says a lot about Isabel's intelligence and abilities that she was trusted with this task. Wives of some of the other men would also remain there when the expedition sailed for the mainland.

Arriving in Cuba, De Soto immediately set to work preparing for the **entrada**, his journey into the unknown. He was determined that his exploration of Florida would be well planned. While he gathered supplies, De Soto trained his men. He settled governing matters. During this time of preparation, he sent Juan de Añasco to explore and map the coast of Florida. He was to look for safe harbors and entry points to the new land.

Añasco returned with better than that. He had captured several Indians. The explorers demanded information from the natives. As would be expected, the Indians did not trust the Spaniards. They were probably willing to say anything to get back home. They told De Soto that there was an abundance of gold in Florida.

De Soto and his men were delighted. They could hardly wait to set sail for this land of riches. Their adventure was soon to begin.

The expedition camps in Florida.

CHAPTER TWO

Florida at Last!

Florida looked lush and green and promising when De Soto first saw it from his ship on May 25, 1539. Excited, he grew impatient during the several days it took to choose a landing site. They needed a harbor deep enough to prevent the ships from scraping bottom. Many experts agree that Tampa Bay was the chosen harbor. Some believe that De Soto landed in the Charlotte Harbor to the south. Differences in compass directions and distances in the written accounts make it difficult for historians to know the exact location.

De Soto went ashore with a small party. He claimed the land of La Florida in the name of the king of Spain. Coming ashore with so few men was risky. Those still on board the ships were too far away to help in case of attack. A strong wind prevented a return to the ships until the next day. But De Soto was lucky. The group saw no Indians this first day.

They had no contact with Indians until after the

remaining men and horses came ashore. The first encounter was not friendly. Several Spaniards met up with Indians armed with bows and arrows. In the fight that followed, two horses and two Indians were killed.

Word spread fast of the Spaniards' presence. Along the coast De Soto saw smoke signals sent up by the Indians. The cruelty of earlier explorers had not been forgotten. Indians deserted their villages. De Soto was unable to capture the local **cacique**, or tribal leader. One of the abandoned villages, Ozita, became the expedition's headquarters. It is believed to have been located near present-day Ruskin, Florida.

To help prevent surprise attacks, De Soto ordered the trees cleared in a wide circle around the camp. The Indians that Añasco had captured escaped. When the Spaniards pursued natives, trying to seize new guides, they found that they were not easy targets. The Indians ran fast—usually too fast to be shot with a **crossbow** or **arquebus**, a heavy matchlock gun. While the Spaniards fumbled with their weapons, the Indians darted about, zinging deadly flint-tipped arrows. Indian arrows penetrated just as deeply as shafts from the Spanish crossbows.

De Soto's men soon learned that their **chain mail** armor provided little or no protection. Indian arrows could easily pierce the metal mesh. The soldiers began

Armor and Weapons

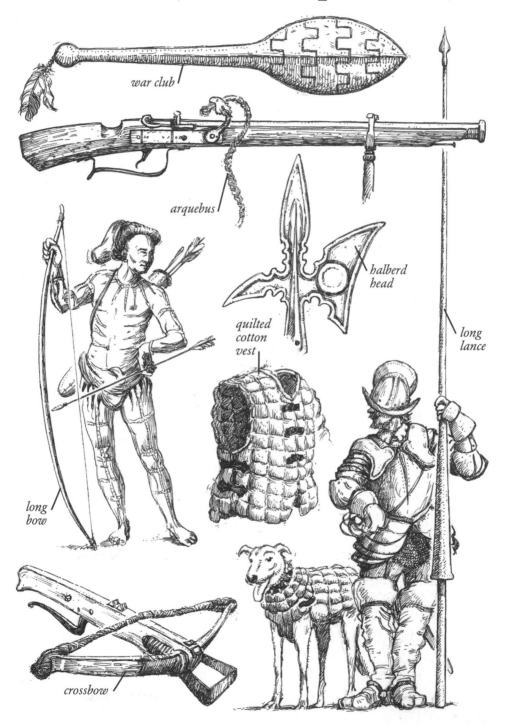

war club

arquebus

halberd
head

quilted
cotton
vest

long
lance

long
bow

crossbow

wearing a thick quilted cotton vest instead. It provided more protection, but guaranteed misery in hot weather.

There were other unhappy discoveries. The Indians could launch a number of arrows in the same time it took a Spaniard to shoot once with the crossbow or arquebus. Some Spanish weapons, like the cannon and the long lance, were designed for European battlefields. They were no good for fighting in wooded areas. They were difficult to haul. For close fighting, the Indians used the war club. The Spaniards found it to be deadly.

The horses gave the Spaniards a big advantage out in the open. On horseback, they could move fast and use their lances. This was the style of battle in which De Soto and his men were experts. But the woods of Florida gave them little room to lunge and retreat. In addition, the trees provided good cover for the Indians. On one occasion an Indian hiding among trees shot two horses ridden by pursuers. As he ran off, the native yelled back, "Let us all fight on foot and we shall see who are the best!"

The Indian guides they finally captured were not interested in helping De Soto. They led the Spaniards into forests and swamps. When the company got mired in quicksand, the guides escaped.

One day, some of De Soto's men happened upon a group of Indians in a clearing and went after them. The natives ran, except for one man. That lone man, who appeared to be an Indian, ran toward them. He cried out in Spanish, "Do not kill me. Do not slay these people. They have given me my life!" He shocked them by making the sign of the cross with his hand and bow.

They had just met Juan Ortiz. He had a fantastic adventure to tell. He had lived with the Indians for twelve years. Ortiz was stranded when the Narváez expedition failed. Captured, he was tortured by the cacique of Ozita. He had many scars to show for it. This cacique had wanted revenge for the brutality he suffered at the hands of the Spaniards. Narváez had cut off the cacique's nose and thrown his mother to the dogs.

The cacique's daughter learned that her father planned to sacrifice Ortiz. She took pity on him. She helped the young man escape to a nearby village of the Timucuan Indians. This tribe was ruled by Mocozo, who gave shelter to the fleeing Spaniard. Ortiz lived with the tribe until he was found by De Soto's men.

De Soto was delighted to have Ortiz in the company. The expedition had gained the best of all interpreters and guides. Not only could Ortiz speak the local native language, he also knew Indian customs. He was familiar with the land around them. As they moved on to areas whose tribes who spoke different tongues, Ortiz would still play a valuable role in the chain of interpreters. He was the guide and advisor that De Soto could most trust.

De Soto immediately asked Ortiz where to find gold. Ortiz answered that he had seen no gold. But the explorer refused to believe that there was none. There had to be gold. He had gambled everything on the possibility of finding treasure. He likely assumed that Ortiz simply had not seen what lay beyond the surrounding area. In addition to his knowledge, Ortiz brought another important gift to De Soto—a friendly contact with Mocozo, the Indian chief who had protected the young man.

De Soto soon met with Mocozo. He must have liked and trusted this cacique. He gave him gifts in thanks for his kindness to Ortiz. And he did not take him hostage, as he did every other cacique along their journey. In fact, he offered to help him against his enemies. He requested—instead of demanding—**porters,** women, and guides.

In spite of De Soto's peaceful approach, Mocozo was probably not pleased with the meeting. De Soto rushed through the elegant formal exchange that was the Indian practice at such meetings. He pushed Mocozo to tell him where silver or gold could be found. As was to become a pattern, Mocozo told him that he might find gold in another province.

Then came good news. Indians from the village of Urriparacoxi told De Soto that a village to the north called Ocale (today's city of Ocala) held all the treasure they could want. The people there were said to wear hats of gold. De Soto might not have believed the entire story, but he undoubtedly hoped that some of it was true. He wanted his men to believe. He wanted them to be eager to move on and explore further.

Leaving some of his men to hold Ozita, De Soto and his company moved northward. Hundreds of Spaniards tramped through the steamy wilderness, loaded down with armor, weapons, and supplies. They drove a herd of pigs and the pack of war dogs. They carried luxury items for De Soto, including a large colorful tent. He had brought grand clothing for meetings with the Indians. But in the hot, humid climate, these luxuries made no sense. The fabrics faded and began to rot.

Most experts think the expedition traveled no more than fifteen miles per day.

It was impossible to carry enough provisions for so many men and animals. There were not enough wild foods along the way to feed more than 600 people. The Spaniards were not skilled hunters. Besides, noise and smells from such a large army would have scared off any game for miles.

De Soto knew that if he could find strong, prosperous **chiefdoms**, their villages would have stored food supplies. From the outset, he had planned to take food from the Indians. He had also planned on capturing Indians to serve as slaves. These slaves would do the hard work of carrying all the gear and feeding his army.

A chiefdom was a small group of natives under one leader. They had little knowledge of the outside world. They provided for themselves and considered outsiders enemies.

Neither of De Soto's plans worked out as expected. They did not find tribes with large quantities of stored food. They were running out of **hardtack** (hard, dry bread) and smoked meat brought from Cuba. Eventually, they were forced to eat roots and cornstalks. The swine were to be killed only for the worst of emergencies. The expedition was not yet at that point, but the men were often hungry.

Many were not happy about having to do their own labor. They had to carry weapons, armor, equipment, and food. They had to grind their own corn and sift it through their chain mail. They had to cook for themselves also. Some, either not willing or not able to do these domestic tasks, ate corn that had not been ground.

The company at last reached Ocale. There, they found some stores of food. But the village was not the rich place the Indians had promised. As usual, the inhabitants had fled before the Spaniards arrived. The cacique sent a message, probably translated by Juan Ortiz. He called the Spaniards vagabonds. He said they traveled to other lands to steal and murder. This cacique did not want peace. He vowed to fight. He said that he and his people would die a thousand deaths to keep their freedom. This confirmed that the Florida Indians were not like those the Spanish had conquered in Peru. Many were willing to die rather than become slaves.

In September, moving farther north, De Soto found that to be true of the natives in Napituca (near present-day Live Oak, Florida). They harassed the Spaniards at every chance. The cacique of this tribe planned a surprise attack, but De Soto got word of the plan. He was ready to respond full force. In this battle, about forty natives were killed. Hundreds were taken prisoner, including the cacique. A small group of survivors took refuge by swimming into the middle of a pond. The Spaniards circled and held it until morning, when the Indians gave up. At that point, the cacique asked for a messenger to take word to his people.

"Go to my people," he said, "and tell them that they take no thought of me." He asked that his people have nothing to do with the Spaniards. Finally, he said, "As for me, if I have to die, it will be as a brave man."

After this conflict, De Soto hoped to move the expedition along. He had obtained the servants he needed and was treating the Indian leader well. He invited the cacique to dine with him. But, in a surprise move during a meal, the cacique landed a violent blow to De Soto's face. He loosened several teeth. Blood gushed. De Soto lost consciousness.

This was the signal every Indian in camp had been waiting for! Two hundred captives leaped up and attacked the Spaniards with pots, plates, burning firewood, or boiling food. Screams of pain filled the camp. The Spaniards suffered many wounds and some casualties, but they managed to put down the revolt. Many Indians were killed, including the cacique. After the uprising, De Soto ordered more of the unarmed captives killed. After this incident, the Spanish began to keep their native prisoners in chains.

> The Indians would have been far more difficult to overcome if most of them had not been kept in chains.

De Soto's men did not feel good about such a massacre. The king of Spain had warned that natives were not to be ill-treated. De Soto himself must have had his doubts. He tried to justify his actions, saying to his men: "If only those Lords of the Council were here so they might see how His Majesty is served in these parts!" The lords of the council were the king's advisors. It was probably safer to blame the advisors than the king.

Yet, his men were not convinced. Most thought he had gone too far. The more hard-hearted considered the executions a waste of needed slaves. This first difference of opinion between De Soto and his men would be a hint of things to come.

Apalachee mound.

CHAPTER THREE

Apalachee

De Soto didn't need the help of Indian guides as the expedition traveled into Apalachee territory. The trail was wide and clear. It had been used by the natives for hundreds of years.

Today's main north-south highways follow Indian trails. The natives used the driest land with the fewest hills and the best places to cross rivers.

The Apalachees were known as the fiercest warriors in the region. They were more advanced than the other Indians De Soto had met. They were the first to have a "Mississippian" organization (see box on page 28). Mississippian chiefdoms were native societies with highly organized systems of agriculture, trade, and defense. The Apalachee cacique ruled over a large fertile region with as many as 100,000 people. In their largest towns, they built mounds and temples.

The Apalachees' fearsome reputation was well deserved. Neighboring tribes avoided fights with them. These were the Indians who had defeated Narváez.

They were not afraid of a new band of Spaniards headed their way.

The Apalachees knew that the horse was the Spaniards' biggest advantage in battle. So they planned to fight in wooded and swampy areas. They decided that if they had to, they would burn their villages and food supplies to keep them from the enemy. If captured, they would not surrender the fight. No matter what, they would not give in.

The Apalachees proved how tough they were in the very first battle. When forced to retreat, they left their village in flames. Some food survived the fire, and De Soto's men gathered all they wanted before dark. Even with full stomachs, the Spaniards could not rest easy. The Apalachees yelled battle cries and shot arrows into

Why Mississippian?

"Mississippian" is a term used to describe advanced chiefdoms of the Mississippi Valley. They were known as the mound builders of the Southeast. These societies were well organized. They grew large amounts of corn and stored it for future needs. They kept armies ready for defense and traded with other chiefdoms. Using baskets of earth and many workers, they built mounds. The tribal chief often lived on top of the highest mound. After the De Soto expedition, no new mounds were constructed.

their camp all night.

After the previous revolt, De Soto was not about to take any chances with Apalachee captives. Prisoners were put in chains and iron collars. In spite of this, some still fought back. Occasionally they managed to kill a Spaniard and escape. Others used sharp rocks to saw off their chains, even though they knew they would be killed if caught trying to escape. Apalachee women could be every bit as fierce as the men. One female captive attacked a Spanish soldier with such a grip that he screamed for mercy.

Under the stress of keeping order and the ongoing battles with the Indians, De Soto grew short-tempered. One soldier left camp without permission. He slipped out to retrieve a sword left along the trail. When he returned, De Soto sentenced the young man to hang. Several top officers pleaded on the young man's behalf. Only then did De Soto cancel the order. The man was probably still punished—beaten or fined for his error.

De Soto kept the company moving until they reached the Apalachee capital, Anhaica. This village was at the site of present-day Tallahassee. There they found a large supply of corn, pumpkins, and other food. This stash would support them through the winter. De Soto put his men to work. They strengthened the walls around the village. He assigned patrols to stand guard

The First Winter Encampment

We know for certain that Anhaica, in present-day Tallahassee, is one site where De Soto camped. In 1987, archaeologist Calvin Jones was studying possible Spanish sites near the state capitol. One day, he saw construction equipment ready to work. He had to act fast. He received permission to dig. Within days, he found Indian and Spanish pottery from the right time period. He dug up rusted handmade nails and bunches of tiny rings—the remains of chain mail. Jones also found a crossbow tip, the jawbone of a pig, and a Portuguese coin. He even found burned remains of corncobs. Luckily, the site had not been disturbed by amateurs or the soon-to-begin construction. Critical information can be lost when proper care is not taken in unearthing artifacts and recording and preserving them.

Portuguese coin

modern copy of chain mail

chain mail fragments

crossbow tip

and alert them to any intruders. Only armed men could go outside the walls to gather food and firewood.

De Soto's men had captured the Apalachee cacique, but he escaped. He got past the guards by crawling along the ground. Embarrassed, the guards told De Soto that the cacique had been lifted into the air and carried away by demons. For once, De Soto was forgiving. He pretended to believe their story and did not punish them.

The Apalachees kept up the raids day and night, growing more fierce in their attacks. Once, they set fire to a large portion of the houses in Anhaica. De Soto tried to behave as if everything was going well. He sent out scouting parties to look for evidence of gold, silver, or other treasure. One of these groups found the place where Narváez and his men built rafts to escape by sea. This site was at an inlet on the Gulf of Mexico the Spaniards had named the Bay of the Horses. There, De Soto's scouts saw the skulls of horses the earlier explorers had killed for food and hides.

> De Soto lived in a time that did not recognize "human rights." His church and his king permitted cruel treatment of unbelievers. Indians practiced cruelty as well. Today such violent acts are unacceptable.

When the scouts returned to camp, they told the eerie story of what they had seen. Many in the expedition began to talk of turning back.

De Soto would put up with no such talk. He sent

Juan de Añasco and thirty men back to Ozita. They were to order the rest of the army to march forward and join the main force. Añasco was to take the ships waiting at Tampa Bay and sail them northward to the Bay of the Horses.

Añasco knew that they would be traveling through dangerous territory. It was winter. They would have to cross frigid waters and brave cold nights. To avoid fighting with the Indians, they would have to race by the villages undetected. Añasco didn't want them to have a chance to mount an attack or to warn other villages. They moved quickly and quietly. The plan worked.

The men from Ozita reached Anhaica without problems. Añasco brought the ships safely up the coast to the Bay of the Horses. Then De Soto sent Francisco Maldonado, one of his most trusted men, to explore the waters of the Gulf Coast. Maldonado was to explore all the coves, inlets, and rivers. He found the harbor De Soto needed and called it Achuse, after the local Indian tribe. This was probably present-day Pensacola Bay.

Winter wore on. De Soto found comfort in reports of gold from captured Indians. One young man excited them with tales of the rumored riches of a country to the northeast. As always, the gold wasn't nearby. This time, the treasure was supposed to be in a province called Cofitachequi, ruled by a woman. The men were so excited that they wanted to head out immediately. But De Soto decided to wait for Maldonado's reports.

When Maldonado returned, De Soto sent him on yet another mission. He was to travel back to Cuba with letters and instructions. This was the last word Isabel would have of her husband for three years.

On March 3, 1540, De Soto left Anhaica and headed north. Most of the men carried their own supplies. Many Indian slaves—underfed, overworked, and forced to sleep on the cold ground—had died during the winter. The **cavalry** (soldiers on horseback) could load their gear on their horses. But the majority of the company was on foot. They had no choice but to carry their loads. They commonly suffered from blisters and

It is estimated that several hundred Indian slaves died over the winter of 1539–40.

sores. It did not seem to occur to De Soto that taking better care of the slaves would have been wise. He would not have to fight new tribes to take more slaves.

The Spaniards traveled into what is now Georgia. The Apalachees allowed them to move on without further warfare. The Indians were probably as exhausted by the

winter of fighting as the Spaniards. With the enemy
leaving their land, they may have felt that they had won.

In this new region, the expedition had less trouble.
They came upon friendly people. The Indians in this
area had probably not met or been mistreated by the
earlier Spaniards. They were willing to get along with
the strangers and offered food and shelter to De Soto's
group.

Feeling like they no longer had to be on the alert for
attacks, the members of the expedition relaxed a little.
The men noticed that the houses of these Indians were
different from those in Florida. Roofs were made of
cane instead of thatched grass. The walls were thicker.
The colder climate required warmer dwellings. In
addition, Georgia provided different building materials
than Florida.

De Soto relaxed, as well. He put on a show with a
cannon for the amazement and entertainment of one
tribe. Of course, he hoped the Indians would be afraid
of this weapon. He wanted them to spread word of the
powerful Spanish army to neighboring tribes.

As a show of friendship, he gave the cacique a small
cannon. This gift was actually not all that generous. The
cacique had no gunpowder, so he was unable to fire the
cannon. With it gone, the Spaniards had one less
burden to carry. In return for this gift, the chief gave

De Soto something much more valuable—a guide. The guide was to lead them to the chiefdom of Cofitachequi.

De Soto had much to think about as he marched with his men toward Cofitachequi. So far, not much had gone according to plan. The treasure they sought was still beyond their reach. They had found no evidence of gold, silver, or jewels. The natives always referred them to other provinces "farther on."

In battle, the Indians had proven that they could not be taken lightly. The Spaniards frequently found themselves at a disadvantage. This was not an easy thought for De Soto. The slaves had proven to be a mixed blessing. Depending on unwilling captives to provide for basic needs had not worked out well. The explorers considered manual labor to be beneath them. But often they had no choice. Even while enslaved and in chains, the Indians had shown that they could do serious harm.

Perhaps the most important thing the Spaniards had learned was that not all native peoples were alike. Because the Peruvian Indians had been fairly easy to subdue, De Soto assumed that others in the New World would be the same. That was a costly mistake. The Indians of La Florida would not surrender. They would not acknowledge the invading Europeans as superior.

Indians were not the simple "heathens" the Spaniards

had expected to find. Often, they showed wisdom, courage, and nobility. The explorers had seen the "savages" display the kind of honor, pride, and bravery that Spaniards held up as ideals.

In spite of these experiences, De Soto's attitude toward the natives did not seem to change. He was probably just relieved that the fierce Indians of the Florida **peninsula** had been left behind.

This historical drawing shows how people once imagined the Lady of Cofitachequi greeting De Soto.

CHAPTER FOUR

Treasure

Near the area that is now Oglethorpe, Georgia, De Soto entered a village and captured several Indians. These men were not as fast as the others who had escaped before the Spaniards arrived. According to Garcilaso de la Vega's account, the natives asked, "Do you wish peace or war?" De Soto claimed he wanted peace.

"It was not necessary to capture us," the Indians told him. "We will give you the supplies that you need… and we will treat you better than they treated you in Apalachee, for we know very well how you fared there."

The Indians kept their word. They ordered food and housing for the expedition. They were lucky—De Soto did not wish to stay long. He was eager to get to Cofitachequi, the land rumored to hold riches. A number of Indians had declared Cofitachequi, ruled by a woman, to be a wealthy province. Some had claimed that the chiefdom had gold.

The men were discontented. They were worn out from walking for miles with heavy loads. The company had been exploring for a year. So far, they had nothing to show for their efforts except sores, losses, and hunger. They didn't share De Soto's enthusiasm for finding this new place. In fact, they were not even sure that they wanted to continue.

When darkness fell, De Soto quietly moved out with a group of noblemen and officers. The next morning, the remaining men realized that he had gone on without them. Greed overcame discontent. Fearing they would lose their share of any found treasure, they gathered up their gear and followed.

The company marched through the area that is present-day Macon, Georgia. They then moved farther north past what is now Milledgeville. They continued to meet peaceful Indians willing to provide food and shelter. Some even gave them meat, which was always scarce unless Indian hunters provided it. The natives' strategy was clearly to get the white men on their way as soon as possible.

De Soto took time to talk to some of the Indians about Christianity. He even put up crosses in two villages, and he read the *requerimiento* to them. Since he took little time to explain it, it would have made no sense to them.

They passed several days in a wilderness. There were

no villages and therefore no food supplies. De Soto ordered the men to eat as little as possible. Several more days went by. They still had found no food. The guides became confused when the trail completely disappeared. To make matters worse, constant rains poured down. The native guides did not know the way to Cofitachequi. They had never been there.

The various chiefdoms frequently had little contact with each other. This was especially true if one province was stronger and could overpower weaker ones near its borders. Cofitachequi was a powerful chiefdom. To prevent trouble, other tribes left a wide **buffer zone** around it. The guides were now far from familiar land.

The buffer zone around Cofitachequi was about 130 miles. This shows how much other provinces feared these Indians.

De Soto was finally forced to order some of the pigs killed. Meat was rationed out, one-half pound per day, per person. The men had to add to that whatever edible leaves and roots they could find. The horses were also hungry, in need of grass or grain. But in the forest, there was little grass and no grain at all.

De Soto sent out scouting parties to look for villages with food. After two days, Juan de Añasco and his party returned. They were loaded down with all the food they could carry—they had found a village. Once there, the men would be able to eat their fill of corn. They could rest and take care of the horses. De Soto stopped slaughtering pigs. These were reserves, only for the times of worst need. Though pigs reproduce fast, it wasn't fast enough to feed an army.

The first meeting between De Soto and the Indians of Cofitachequi occurred near what is present-day Camden, South Carolina. The natives came forward to greet the Spaniards. They brought gifts and welcomed the expedition with speeches.

The Spaniards were impressed with the tribe's young leader. She was beautiful and gracious. They called her *La Señora de Cofitachequi*: the Lady of Cofitachequi. The Lady presented De Soto with a large string of pearls and accepted a ruby ring from him. She allotted half the houses in her village for their use. Her people had endured a **plague**, she explained. Many had died. The empty dwellings were sad evidence of their recent suffering.

The Lady told the explorers that her food supplies were not as plentiful as usual. In spite of this, she promised to share what she had: turkeys, dried venison, corn, walnuts, and mulberries. She also gave them blankets and furs.

De Soto showed little interest in these gifts. He rushed to ask her his burning question—did the province have any gold or silver? He and his men pointed to their rings to make sure she understood. To their delight, she answered yes. She immediately sent for samples to show them. De Soto was deeply disappointed to find that the Cofitachequi "gold" was only copper. Their "silver" was actually mica.

It is likely that the young cacique of Cofitachequi recognized De Soto's disappointment. She would not have missed his interest when he spotted pearls. Generously, she told him he could have all the pearls he wanted. They could be found in the mortuary house, the final resting place of their dead. There were more pearls there than he could haul away, she promised.

De Soto and his secretary Rodrigo Rángel soon visited these temples, houses of the dead. Boxes that held the corpses were filled with pearls. But most of the pearls had been ruined, blackened by the fire used to open the oyster shells. They were also damaged by red-hot wires used to drill holes in them. The long contact with bones and decay hadn't helped, either. Rángel thought that he had found an emerald among the pearls. He showed it to De Soto, who was pleased. But the stone turned out to be only a glass bead.

The Lady of Cofitachequi urged still more pearls

upon De Soto, but he said no. He had as much as he could carry. But there was something else he wanted. De Soto had discovered that the Lady's mother was still living. He was determined to meet her. Perhaps he thought the older woman might have gold or knowledge of where other treasure could be found. We do not know his exact motives.

He sent out search parties to locate her, but she eluded him. She also sent messages to her daughter. She scolded the Lady for meeting with the Spaniards and helping them. De Soto finally sent Juan de Añasco out with a guide who knew exactly where the old woman was. The young man was caught between the Lady's order to take the Spaniards to her mother and the certain anger of the old woman if he led them there. On the way, he stabbed and killed himself with an arrow. De Soto gave up the search.

In addition to pearls, De Soto made another discovery while in the house of the dead—Spanish relics from the explorer Ayllón's expedition. He found an iron ax and rosary beads. Like De Soto, Ayllón had come to this land seeking riches.

The friendliness of the Indians and the beauty of the land convinced many of De Soto's men that they should start a colony in Cofitachequi. After all, they had failed to find gold after many months of marching, fighting, and near-starvation.

At this point the land seemed treasure enough. But De Soto was not interested. He listened to their opinions, but decided to move on. If they did not find the riches they sought, he promised them that they could return to Cofitachequi in the future.

On May 13, 1540, as the expedition prepared to move out, trouble started. None of the chronicles say exactly what happened. Offenses had been committed against the Indians. Whatever the Spaniards had done, the Lady and her people were angry.

Word got to De Soto that she might refuse to provide guides, interpreters, and carriers. This he could not risk. He acted quickly. He took the Lady hostage. She was forced to give him whatever he demanded. Outwardly, De Soto and the rest of the company showed her courtesy, but no one was fooled. Everyone knew that she was a prisoner.

The expedition marched to the northwest. Indians they met along the way were peaceful. As they traveled, the Spaniards saw fewer cornfields. The horses were again growing thin. At that point, a hurricane ripped through, pounding them with high winds and large hailstones. It took two days to recover from the storm. Soon after, they crossed the Blue Ridge Mountains.

These mountains are part of the Appalachians, near the present-day border between North Carolina and Tennessee. The mountains marked the outer boundary of the province of Cofitachequi.

When the Lady realized that she was being taken out of her territory, she was alarmed. Her people could not help her if she was outside her own province. Members of other tribes would have no loyalty to her. They might enslave or even kill her.

Pretending that she had to relieve herself in the woods, she slipped away from the main group. Escaping, she took with her some of the most valuable pearls. Since she had plenty of pearls at home, it is obvious that she did this to punish the Spaniards. She had given generously from all she had. In exchange, she had been taken prisoner and her people used. Her mother's cautions about dealings with the white men had been well-founded. The Lady could not be certain if her people would welcome her back. They may have felt that she betrayed them.

Both Rodrigo Rángel and the Gentleman from Elvas were critical of De Soto's treatment of the Lady.

This was a sad ending to an encounter with people who had shown the Spaniards every kindness. Since the expedition might later return to Cofitachequi, one would think that De Soto would have made an effort to remain on good terms with its people and its beautiful ruler. But his behavior clearly shows, once again, his firm belief in the conquistador's right to use the natives to serve his own ends. The people of Cofitachequi had been nothing more than pawns in his quest for wealth and glory.

Another Spaniard Visits Cofitachequi

In 1566, Juan Pardo arrived in Cofitachequi territory. He was scouting for potential settlement locations along the Carolina coast. He also sought a route to New Spain—Mexico. When he visited Cofitachequi, it was no longer a thriving province. In only twenty-six years, the chiefdom had fallen apart. Towns were nearly empty. Farmland was abandoned. The gracious Lady of Cofitachequi and most of her people were gone.

The chief of the Coosa Indians.

CHAPTER FIVE

Marching through Coosa

De Soto marched through the area that is now western North Carolina and eastern Tennessee. Some men reported seeing "signs of gold" in the mountains. Scholars think it is possible that they found gold dust in the mountain streams. If so, that was not enough to make

> In 1820, gold was discovered in this area by a farmer named John Reed. There also were deposits of copper. De Soto did not pause to find either.

De Soto stop. He wanted to find gold already mined and collected. Besides, the need for food was urgent and the Indians in the mountains were so poor that there was little to steal.

Some of the men no longer agreed with De Soto's goals. They were tired of forced marches and strict rules. They probably thought that they could fend for themselves and find enough food. They wanted to stop to look for gold. Several men deserted. Two were captured and brought back to face a furious De Soto.

One of the chronicles says that De Soto wanted to hang the deserters. It is not clear whether they were hung as a warning to others.

The expedition crossed into what many scholars think was Cherokee land. These Indians gave them food and helped carry their supplies to Chiaha. This village is believed to have been near present-day Newport, Tennessee (east of Knoxville). The Spaniards stopped in Chiaha to rest. They were again without food. The horses were too weak to carry riders. The Indians provided them a variety of things to eat—bear fat, honey, walnuts, and acorns. There was plenty of grass, too. The horses had a chance to rest, graze, and recover their strength.

As had become his practice, De Soto insulted the goodwill of his hosts. He requested thirty females. That very night, the men of Chiaha ran off, taking the women and children. The chief soon surrendered. Forcing him to be a guide, De Soto and his men searched the area. They even chopped down the corn growing around the village.

But it was no use—the women were not to be found. Only when De Soto agreed to cancel his request did the families return. Probably to hurry the Spaniards out, the chief ordered 500 of his people to serve as porters. They were to carry the expedition's gear to the next province.

De Soto directed his men south, toward the Gulf of Mexico. He probably planned to meet his ships at Achuse to restock his supplies. He had no gold, but at least he could show the Cofitachequi pearls. He could tell the men on board about the rumors of gold and copper. Certainly, he would make the most of the signs of gold they had seen in the mountains.

In early summer, De Soto reached Coste. Like most other natives in the area, the Indians of Coste welcomed them. Once again, De Soto abused their hospitality. His men stole corn from the cacique's supply. It took playacting by De Soto to save them from a battle for which they were not prepared. De Soto pretended to punish the thieves. He struck the men, whispering to them to play along. Once he calmed the Indians, De Soto led the cacique away from his guards, as if to speak with him in private. He then ordered him to be taken prisoner.

In June, De Soto crossed the northern border of Coosa territory. It isn't certain where the capital was located. Many believe it was near present-day Carters, Georgia. Sixteenth-century European artifacts have been discovered in that area. Items recovered include iron tools. A double-edged sword believed to date to the mid-1500s was dug up nearby.

As the expedition neared the capital, De Soto was given a royal welcome. The chief came out to meet him. He was seated regally on a chair carried on the shoulders of his advisors. He was surrounded by Indians singing and playing flutes. The cacique ordered that a town be emptied to house the Spaniards.

De Soto responded by taking the cacique and his sister prisoner. He then made his usual demands of food, porters, guides, and women. Holding the two captives guaranteed that all his requests were obeyed. When they saw their chief in chains, most of the natives ran into the woods. De Soto's men pursued them. They chained those they captured. This probably added several hundred slaves to the expedition.

Some scholars think this move by De Soto is what led to the Spaniards' later troubles. The Coosa chief was important. When news of his ill-treatment reached other chiefdoms, they realized that kindness was useless in dealing with the Spaniards. Their generosity did not result in their being treated fairly in return. The Indians probably decided to work together to defeat the white invaders.

On August 20, 1540, De Soto led the expedition through heavy rains to Itaba. This is believed to be at present-day Cartersville, Georgia, site of the Etowah Mounds. Here, the Spaniards traded mirrors and knives for Indian women.

About a week later, they marched on to Ulibahali, believed to be near Rome, Georgia. Indians in this village were angry when they saw their leader being held prisoner. They showed signs of wanting to attack. But the cacique, perhaps fearing a bloody defeat, ordered them to put down their weapons.

When they left the province, De Soto freed the cacique. But he refused to release the man's sister. The cacique was angry at being taken such a distance from his home. He had been humiliated. He was heartbroken at losing his sister. This proud Indian leader was reduced to tears.

Following the Coosa River, the expedition continued south. On September 16th, they reached Talisi. This village was near the site of present-day Childersburg, Alabama. De Soto received messengers from Tascaluza, a well-known cacique. Tascaluza ruled the province of Atahachi, which they were nearing. De Soto had already heard of this powerful, fierce chiefdom. He may have been expecting the contact.

Not long after, Tascaluza's son arrived to meet De Soto. Hoping to frighten or impress the young man, De Soto ordered his cavalry to mount their horses. Others sounded trumpets. The records don't say if this bullying tactic worked, but it is doubtful.

The two men spoke. It was agreed that De Soto would send two men to Tascaluza. They would take one trail going and a different trail back. This way, they could decide which was the best route to Atahachi.

The company rested. Two weeks later, they began moving southward. They probably passed near what is now Sylacauga, Alabama. They camped at Uxapita (near Wetumpka). Then, only a league away from Atahachi (present-day Montgomery), De Soto sent word to Tascaluza that he had arrived. A return message came from the chief. He invited De Soto to meet with him whenever he was ready.

De Soto was ready—or thought he was.

Who's Who?

Scholars are not sure which tribes occupied various provinces. Cherokees, Creeks, and Seminoles lived in the area. De Soto wasn't interested in learning about the natives. A century later, colonists began to record those facts. By that time, many tribal groups had migrated to different locations. Some blended with other tribes. Others died out due to diseases such as smallpox and measles. These diseases were brought to the New World by Europeans and they devastated the native population.

Seminole beadwork

Creek weaving

Cherokee pottery

Chief Tascaluza travels to Mabila.

CHAPTER SIX

Facing Tascaluza

When De Soto arrived at the Atahachi capital, Tascaluza was waiting for him. The cacique was in front of his house. Seated on a mat, he was surrounded by

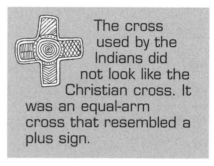

The cross used by the Indians did not look like the Christian cross. It was an equal-arm cross that resembled a plus sign.

advisors and servants. One of the men sheltered the chief with a sunshade marked with a white cross. Tascaluza was a giant of a man, about a foot-and-a-half taller than the tallest of the Spaniards. He held himself with the kind of dignity that was fitting for one who ruled over many chiefdoms.

They spoke through interpreters. De Soto was not able to take charge as he liked to at such meetings. Suddenly, Luis de Moscoso and some other men jumped on their horses. They galloped about, charging this way and that, sometimes appearing to charge directly toward Tascaluza.

It was the same tactic that De Soto had tried with Atahualpa a few years earlier in Peru. Tascaluza was no more impressed than the Inca king had been. He pretended lack of interest. Tascaluza watched the performance only part of the time. He seemed to be bored. De Soto moved closer and took Tascaluza's hand. The cacique did not respond. He remained dignified and calm.

De Soto finally swallowed his pride. He sat down and acted as if everything was as it should be. They talked for a time. Then the chief invited the Spaniards to eat. As they ate, some Indians danced. Things seemed to be going along pleasantly, but then De Soto broke the good mood. He demanded porters and women.

Tascaluza's response was icy. He was not accustomed to serving others, he said. In fact, others served him.

Angry, De Soto ordered that Tascaluza be taken hostage. The cacique was to sleep where De Soto slept. He would be under guard at all times. When De Soto again demanded porters and women, Tascaluza agreed to cooperate. He said he would give him the porters right away, but could not turn over the women yet. The women would be provided when they reached a place called Mabila.

Perhaps to further intimidate the cacique, De Soto ordered a horse for Tascaluza. Tascaluza made no protest about riding the fearsome beast. Finding a mount big enough for so large a man wasn't easy. Even on one of the largest packhorses, his feet almost reached the ground.

They headed out. Moving along the southern bank of the Alabama River, they made a stop at Piachi, believed to be near present-day Selma, Alabama. The Spaniards began to notice defiance from the Indians. When De Soto demanded a canoe, the chief of Piachi told him they had none. De Soto's men were forced to build rafts to cross the river. This took time. Delay was probably what the Indians had in mind.

As they traveled farther, two of the soldiers disappeared. De Soto demanded that they be returned. He threatened to burn Tascaluza at the stake. Tascaluza promised the return of the men at Mabila. Other Indians were less agreeable. When they were asked about the missing men, they sarcastically asked if they were the Spaniards' keepers.

The company was nearing Mabila. Tascaluza sent a messenger ahead, supposedly to order food, porters, and women for the Spaniards. De Soto sent his own scouts ahead to find out what was going on at Mabila. Those men returned a day later with bad news. Many Indians were gathered in the town. They were armed. Messengers also came back to Tascaluza. They brought him food and were almost certainly giving him reports, as well.

De Soto felt the need to be cautious. On the morning of October 18, 1540, he led the way to Mabila with forty horsemen. The men on horseback were backed by others armed with crossbows and **halberds**. Porters went with them, carrying supplies. As they marched past Indian towns, many soldiers fell behind. They were looking for food or other goods they could steal.

It was still early morning when De Soto arrived at Mabila. It was a walled village, surrounded by a wooden **palisade**. The wall was made of side-by-side posts, bound together with cane and plastered with mud and straw. Every fifty feet, there were raised sections that made platforms on which Indians could stand and shoot arrows. Narrow openings in the wall between the raised sections allowed shooting from inside. There were two gates, one to the east and one to the west. The town had a central plaza. Houses were built in a circle around the plaza.

De Soto's officers were alarmed. The Indians were preparing for battle. Scouts had seen Indians carrying weapons inside the gates. They had seen them performing what looked like military exercises. The walls had been recently reinforced. All the trees and bushes had been cleared for a great distance around the village. The officers also noted that the Indians in Mabila were mostly young warriors and leaders. They had seen no servants, and the few women present were all young. They had at that point seen no children. In other words,

The village of Mabila.

this did not look like an ordinary Indian village.

Still, the Indians were agreeable. Several high-ranking natives politely asked De Soto if he would prefer to camp outside or inside the town. Despite the advice of his officers, De Soto chose to stay inside. He said he was tired of sleeping in the open.

The cacique of Mabila came to greet them. He brought along a crowd of Indians who sang and chanted. De Soto seemed to relax. He and a number of his men tied their horses at the gate. They entered the village on foot. The Indians walked with them, singing. Young attractive Indian women danced for them.

Tascaluza chose this time to tell De Soto that he would go no farther. He would stay in Mabila when the expedition moved on. De Soto replied that Tascaluza would not be allowed to stay. Saying he needed to talk with the other chiefs, Tascaluza turned away. He went into one of the large houses before anyone could stop him.

De Soto sent Juan Ortiz after him, but Tascaluza would not come out. His next words were chilling. De Soto could leave in peace now. If he did not, he and the other chiefs would force him to leave.

No doubt it infuriated De Soto to have a savage speak to him in this insulting way. He sent Baltasar de Gallegos to order Tascaluza outside. Entering the house,

Gallegos saw that it was full of men armed for battle. Right away, he sounded a cry of alarm. De Soto put on his helmet. He told his men to get to their horses and warn the others outside the gate.

Tascaluza had the advantage. Suddenly, De Soto was willing to make a deal. He called out to one of the chiefs that Tascaluza could remain in Mabila if he would provide a guide and porters for the expedition. The man refused to carry the message. Gallegos grabbed the chief's robe, but he slipped out of it and kept on walking. Enraged, Gallegos drew his sword and sliced off one of the man's arms.

It was like striking a match. A mighty roar rose from the thousands of Indian warriors inside the walls. Armed Indians poured from every building. Arrows flew from every direction. De Soto and his men retreated, leaving the porters behind. They fought their way toward the gate. De Soto fell several times, but managed to get up and continue fighting.

His thoughts must have been racing. He knew he couldn't order his cavalry inside and risk losing the horses. He yelled to the men outside the gate to fall back to a safe distance. He knew that his entire army had not yet arrived.

Many of the men had no time to mount. Some could only cut their horses loose so the animals could escape danger. Some men could not even do that. The Indian porters still outside the gate immediately took the Spaniards' weapons and supplies inside the walls. They joined the fight against De Soto and his men.

At this important moment, the rest of De Soto's army arrived. De Soto was never more brilliant than when backed into a corner and outnumbered. Quickly, he divided his men into four groups. He sent them to attack the four sides of the town. They were to kill anyone who tried to escape. They were to set fire to the town.

The Indians fought desperately to keep the Spanish out, but it was hopeless. Houses burst into flames. De Soto's men raced their horses through breaks in the wall and rode through the village, lancing Indians as they went. As De Soto rose to thrust his lance, an arrow caught him in the left buttock. He had to endure the rest of the battle standing in the stirrups.

The whole town became a huge roaring fire. Indians who tried to escape were either slaughtered or driven back into the flames. Many threw themselves into burning buildings rather than be taken alive. A few managed to escape, but with terrible injuries. Probably few survived. Indian women and even small boys picked up the weapons of the dead warriors and fought alongside the men. When the last warrior saw that he had no hope, he hung himself with his bow string.

The Spaniards won—but at what cost? They had lost practically everything. Gone were their weapons, clothing, medical supplies, and the Cofitachequi pearls. The wine and wafers the priests used in saying Mass had also been destroyed. This loss was frightening to men who believed their souls were in danger if they could not observe the sacraments in the proper way. The Spaniards even lost their playing cards—no small loss for men who often had time on their hands. Forty-seven men died, and hundreds were injured. They lost forty-five horses.

> Rodrigo Rángel stayed by De Soto's side and rescued him more than once. Afterward, De Soto pulled more than twenty arrows from Rángel's quilted cotton armor.

The Indians lost far more. Beyond the massive number of dead, they lost centuries of knowledge carried by those who died—how to grow food, how to construct buildings, how to govern, how to treat illnesses. Much of the culture of several tribes vanished that day. Some scholars believe that the Indians who fought at Mabila came from many chiefdoms. They had come together to defeat the Spaniards. Many provinces experienced devastating losses in addition to those under Tascaluza's rule.

Some Indian women captured after the fight at Mabila said that Tascaluza began to plan the battle as soon he heard about De Soto. Others said he planned it as revenge after he learned how badly De Soto had treated the cacique of Coosa.

After Mabila, De Soto was a changed man. Before that battle, he had decided to meet his ships at Achuse. He would give them the pearls as proof of his success. He was beginning plans for establishing a colony. Now he couldn't meet the ships—not as a defeated man—a man with a tattered army and no treasure.

De Soto also knew that his men would abandon the expedition if they could get to the ships. Rumors of their growing discontent had reached his ears. Some of the men who had originally been his firmest supporters, like Juan Gaytan, wanted to head for the ships. He and others were ready to end the expedition.

De Soto felt betrayed. He would no longer consider his men's advice or opinions. He refused to give up. In his view, pushing on offered the only hope for success. There was still a chance that his great gamble could pay off. He could not face going back to a life of poverty in Spain.

In spite of his pride and stubbornness, De Soto knew that he was to blame for the tragedy of Mabila. He had refused to listen to warnings that the Indians were preparing for battle. He led his men inside the village walls. He had allowed Tascaluza to slip away into the house. And he had allowed the slaves carrying their all-important supplies to venture too close to the gate.

The body of Tascaluza's son was found but not that of Tascaluza himself. He may have been burned beyond recognition. It is possible that he escaped.

None of the chronicles say how De Soto convinced his men to continue on. He may have told them that there wasn't enough food available to the south. There is a chance that he convinced them, once more, that gold lay ahead. But it is hard to imagine that worn-out promise swaying the battle-weary men. Whatever method he used, he somehow convinced them to go on. After resting and tending to their wounds, the company headed northwest instead of south toward the ships.

De Soto crosses the Tombigbee River.

CHAPTER SEVEN

On to the Great River

Leaving Mabila, many in the expedition were still suffering from the wounds of that battle. Food supplies were low. The weather was cold and rainy. They arrived fairly quickly at Apafalaya, near present-day Moundville, Alabama. Along the way, they skirmished several times with Indians who did not willingly give up their corn. These fights further weakened the already-exhausted soldiers.

They crossed the Tombigbee River into what is now Mississippi. Soon they came to an abandoned village of the Chicaza Indians. They decided to winter there, even though there were not enough houses for everyone. Many men had to sleep outside on snow-covered ground. For the poorly clothed travelers, the winter cold was an extreme hardship. The Spaniards

The Indian slaves had no shelter from rain, cold, or snow. They were underfed and poorly clothed. As a result, many died during the winter months.

found and tore down empty Indian dwellings in the area. They used the materials to build more shelters in the village.

At first, De Soto got along fairly well with the Chicaza Indians nearby. He entertained the chief and other important guests with a pork dinner. The Indians liked the pork. They were probably near starvation. Most of their corn had been taken by the Spaniards. Indians began to sneak into the camp at night to steal pigs. The Spaniards caught three of the thieves. De Soto executed two. He ordered the hands of the third cut off. The man was sent back to his tribe. It was hoped this would discourage further stealing. Ironically, De Soto felt justified in punishing the Indians for stealing, even though he regularly took food from them.

Members of the expedition continued to steal food and other items from the natives. As tensions grew, De Soto ordered his men to leave the Indians alone. A few ignored the orders and stole skins from the Chicazas. De Soto then ordered the thieves to be executed. He refused to listen to pleas for mercy. When the Indians arrived demanding justice, Ortiz deliberately mistranslated their message. He told De Soto that the Chicazas were asking him to spare the men's lives. De Soto agreed.

In March 1541, as De Soto was preparing to move

out, he demanded 200 porters from the cacique. The Indians were very upset. But the cacique promised that the porters would be delivered on March 4th, the day they were to leave.

On the night of the 3rd, De Soto saw clues that the Indians were up to something. He told his men, "Tonight is an Indian night." He ordered that extra caution be taken. He would sleep with his weapons nearby. His horse would be saddled and ready.

The men seemed to ignore De Soto's warnings. None had his horse saddled. No one had weapons close at hand. Perhaps they were so weary they thought only of sleep. That night, Moscoso had assigned the least capable men to guard duty. Indian spies knew exactly where those worthless guards were. And for some reason, the usually alert dogs, pigs, and horses made no sound.

So, while the Spaniards slept, more than 300 Indians sneaked into camp. They carried covered jars containing fire. They shot flaming arrows into the dwellings. Over half the houses were burning before the Spaniards knew what was happening. Whipped by a strong north wind, the fire quickly spread. The camp filled with smoke. War whoops and Indian drums were heard. The terrified guards ran away.

The Spaniards burst out of the burning houses half-dressed, without weapons. They came face to face with the waiting Indians. Some ran. Horses able to escape their reins bolted.

In the confusion, only De Soto and one other man were able to mount their horses. The smoke made it hard to see. The Indians heard riderless horses stampeding through the smoke and fire. They thought that a large number of Spaniards on horseback were charging them. Racing out of the camp, they headed for the safety of the woods.

Twelve Spaniards died in the attack. Others were so badly wounded that they had to be carried on stretchers when the expedition moved on. Fifty-seven horses and over 400 pigs were lost. Only piglets small enough to crawl through gaps in the pens survived.

Nearly all their remaining clothing was destroyed in the fire. The soldiers had lost most of their weapons and saddles. The only death on the Indian side was one man De Soto killed. That night, the Spaniards suffered a complete defeat at the hands of the Chicazas.

The Indians planned to attack again the following night. But it rained. The rain soaked their bowstrings, making them slack. They were forced to cancel their plans, since their weapons were useless wet. If they had been able to attack again within twenty-four hours, they most likely would have completely crushed the Spaniards.

Over the following days, the men treated their wounds. They made clothing out of deerskins. They had to resort to the dead horses for food. A forge was constructed to temper and repair weapons damaged in the fire. New shields were formed from bear hides. They carved new lances from the wood of ash trees.

It was past mid-April when the expedition at last moved out, headed northwest. As usual, they were in need of food. When they found a well-defended Alibamo Indian palisade, De Soto decided he had no choice. He would show the jeering Indians inside that he wasn't afraid to take them on.

They lost fifteen men taking the palisade and killed three Indians—all for nothing. There was no food or anything else of value inside the walls. The palisade had only been built to fool the Spaniards! De Soto's men blamed him for being taken in by this trick.

The need for food was so great that they had to move on. The wounded had no time to heal. Those on stretchers were dying as the expedition traveled. De Soto headed for what is today the northwestern part of Mississippi. In early May, the company arrived at a Quizquiz village. Most of the men of the village were away, so the Spaniards easily made off with animal skins and slaves.

De Soto sent word to the chief that if he would come in peace the Spaniards would return all they had taken. The chief replied that De Soto must give up what he had taken first, and then they would meet. De Soto returned the goods, but the chief still refused to meet with him. This time, De Soto wasn't up to a fight. The expedition moved on to other Quizquiz villages, where they found supplies of corn.

In May of 1541, they reached the Mississippi River. De Soto may not have been as impressed with the great river as we might think. There is a famous painting of this event in which the governor and his men are shown wearing velvets, taffetas, armor, and helmets. The horses are sleek and well fed. They are portrayed as they looked when they first arrived in La Florida. This painting is pure fantasy—by this time, fine clothing was nothing but a memory. As for the great river, it was just one more obstacle to overcome. They set up camp and began to build boats for the crossing.

A dugout was a canoe made from a single log. The inside of the vessel was burned out.

A few days later, Indians showed up in very large dugout canoes. They announced that their cacique, Aquijo, would come the following day. The cacique did arrive, with several thousand Indians armed with bows and arrows. Seeing so many warriors probably made De Soto nervous, but he didn't show it. In fact, De Soto invited the cacique to come ashore.

Aquijo had probably heard how the Spaniards took native leaders hostage. He sent gifts, but kept his distance. Again, De Soto asked the chief to come ashore. Instead, the canoes drew back. Somehow, this alarmed the crossbowmen. They began shooting. Several Indians fell, but the canoes kept moving away in military order. When out of range of Spanish arrows, the Indians jeered. Then they left. That wasn't to be the end of it.

Every day, the Indians returned to see how the Spaniards were progressing with the boats. Arrows were exchanged. Little damage was done on either side. Finally, early the morning of June 18th, horses and men set out across the river aboard four wooden barges.

Reaching the opposite shore safely, they continued on into land that is now Arkansas. They found and robbed a Casqui village. The natives there approached De Soto peacefully. They had heard of the Spaniards' God.

> When they safely reached the other side of the Mississippi River, De Soto had his men tear the boats apart. They pulled out and saved every nail and spike.

They asked questions about the Christian faith. The province was suffering a long drought. Desperate, they asked the Spaniards to pray to their God for rain. De Soto ordered one of his carpenters to build a cross out of pine poles. When it was finished, they set it up on a mound high above the river. Spaniards and Indians lined up behind the priests. They marched together to the cross and prayed.

That very night it rained.

The Casquis now believed in the magic of the Spaniards and their God. The chief asked De Soto to join them in fighting their enemies in the village of Pacaha. De Soto and his soldiers did this. He and his men stole corn, cloth, and skins from the defeated village. But trouble started when the Casqui chief kept some of the Pacaha goods that De Soto wanted.

A year or two earlier, De Soto might have let a conflict like this pass. But since Mabila, he didn't always use good judgment. He sent a group of men on revenge raids on the Casqui. He then offered to help Pacaha fight Casqui. The Casqui leader found out and immediately offered to hand over the stolen items. He again expressed a desire for peace.

While playing the two chiefs against each other, De Soto sent out scouting parties. He had to decide which direction the expedition should go. His choices were running out. To the east there were only tribes he had fought and alienated. To the south were more villages like those he had already visited. The land to the north was thinly populated. It would provide little or no food.

To the west was a stretch of wilderness. He was told that on the other side of that forest lived a tribe of buffalo hunters. So it was decided. They would head west. De Soto still carried some hope of finding riches in unknown lands.

The expedition leaves North America.

CHAPTER EIGHT

De Soto Loses Hope

The expedition traveled past the lower St. Francis River in what is now Arkansas. By this time there was much tension and strain between De Soto and his men. Many were bitter about the march inland. They would have preferred to return to the ships anchored in the Gulf (at what is now Pensacola Bay). One night, De Soto heard that Juan Gaytan refused to take his assigned watch. He lost control. He shouted loudly enough for the entire camp to hear, accusing the men of plotting and cowardice. He declared, "For as long as I live, no one is to leave this land before we have conquered and settled it or all died in the attempt!"

The Spaniards traveled farther northwest. They stopped briefly at Coligua near the site of present-day Batesville, Arkansas. They then moved on to Cayas. The Indians there raised corn and traded in salt, but had no treasure. After a few weeks, De Soto made a fateful decision—to visit the Tula Indians to the west.

He took a Tula village by surprise but these Indians were ready to fight. They lost a number of men but wounded a few Spaniards in return. The Tulas used long lances with sharp points for killing buffalo. These hunter-warriors were not afraid of horses—they quickly figured out how to use their weapons against the animals. This made them a dangerous enemy. De Soto could not afford to lose any more horses.

Since the entrada began, De Soto had lost 250 men and 150 horses.

After a number of battles, De Soto reached an uneasy truce with the Tulas. Winter was approaching. De Soto knew he needed to find a place to spend the cold months. He reversed his path, heading southeast. The expedition finally stopped at Utiangue, in the area that is now Little Rock. The town had plentiful stocks of food. De Soto and his men fortified the outer walls to protect against attacks. Every so often, he created false alarms. He wanted to see how fast the men could be ready to fight.

In March 1542, the expedition moved on to Anilco and then to Guachoya. Despite the failures of the past three years, De Soto still hoped to find a wealthy Indian province somewhere. He questioned the cacique of Guachoya and was told that there were no such provinces. He refused to believe this. There had to be a

rich village. He sent Juan de Añasco down the
Mississippi to investigate. When Añasco returned, he
confirmed what the cacique had said. There were no
wealthy villages.

De Soto's dream of New World treasure finally
ended. There were no riches here like the Inca gold the
conquistadors had found in Peru. This new land would
not reward his efforts. About the time De Soto realized
this, he fell ill, probably with malaria or typhoid.

In the swampy river terrain, mosquitoes were
abundant. The Spaniards suffered from painful bites.
They had no idea that the insects could carry diseases
that could kill them.

Though sick, De Soto still had to deal with the
Indians. He sent a message to the chief of the powerful
Quigualtam kingdom claiming to be the Child of the

A Great Loss

Among those who died during the winter of 1541–1542
was Juan Ortiz. He dreamed of returning home to Spain,
but his journey ended in an unmarked grave somewhere
in present-day Arkansas. When the expedition moved out,
they no longer had a dependable translator. Without his
skills, they had to travel more slowly and carefully.

Sun. He demanded that the cacique come to Guachoya and bring a gift of whatever was most valuable. Perhaps this was De Soto's one last attempt to get gold.

The message sent back said that if De Soto would dry up the Mississippi River, the cacique would believe that he was a god. He also said that people came to visit him and to pay him tribute. If they did not, he forced them to do so. De Soto should come to him. If the Spaniard came in peace, he would be welcomed. If he arrived armed, Quigualtam would be prepared to fight.

De Soto was furious at this reply but too sick to respond. The fever had him, and he had to rest often. He also heard rumors that the Indians were planning an attack. The expedition was not prepared for battle. Their walled village did not even have gates. De Soto had refused to build any. He thought this action might cause the Indians to think the Spaniards were afraid. Instead, he posted extra guards.

To show their strength, De Soto decided they should attack a local tribe. Not Quigualtam or Guachoya—they were too powerful. He sent men out to attack Anilco, ordering that no male was to be spared. More than a hundred were killed. Braves from Guachoya were invited to go with the Spaniards. They were to report what they saw to inspire fear in others.

De Soto grew more ill. When he realized that death

*De Soto died on May 21, 1542, about one year
after he first saw the Mississippi River.*

was near, he called his top officers to his bedside.
Thanking them, he requested their prayers. He asked
them to pardon his mistakes. He made out a new will
and had it read. In an earlier will, he had remembered
two illegitimate children—a boy and a girl. Since he had

no children from his marriage to Isabel, it is likely that he included them. He left bequests to his family, some friends, and his loyal secretary, Rodrigo Rángel.

De Soto told his men to elect a new leader. Instead, they asked that he appoint the man who would take command. De Soto chose Luis de Moscoso. The men swore to obey him.

De Soto died the next day, May 21, 1542. Some were glad he was gone. After three years of suffering and no reward, they had lost faith in their leader. One of the chronicles said, "they [the men] did not visit him and wait upon him as was fitting." Now they could end their misery and go home.

The first priority was to keep the Indians from knowing that De Soto was dead. He had presented himself as an immortal deity. With him gone, the Indians might think that the Spaniards were helpless. So, in the darkness of night, De Soto's men secretly buried him just inside the camp walls.

But the Indians had known that De Soto was sick. When they no longer saw him, they suspected he was dead. They noticed loose soil over the poorly concealed grave. A few days later, under the cover of night, the Spaniards dug up De Soto's body. They weighted the body with sand, placed it in a canoe, and rowed out to the middle of the river. De Soto was sent to his final

resting place in the depths of the Mississippi. The
Indians were later told that De Soto had gone to visit
the sky.

Moscoso called a meeting. They all wanted to end
the expedition. They had to decide whether to build
boats and sail down the Mississippi and on to Mexico
or Cuba, or to go overland to Mexico. There was still
the possibility of discovering riches on the way. Building
boats would take a long time. They didn't know what
dangers they might find on the river. There could be
rapids or waterfalls. If they went overland, they could
leave immediately. They decided to go by land.

The expedition headed out on June 5, 1542. They
fought and stole their way across land that is present-day
Arkansas and Texas. They may have gone as far as the
Brazos River. The terrain got drier and drier as they
went. They saw few Indian tribes. The Indians they did
find were hunters who grew no corn. The Spaniards
needed large amounts of corn to survive.

By October, they had to face the fact that another
winter would soon be upon them. Moscoso and the
men decided to return to the Great River. There, at least,
they knew they could find natives with corn. They
would go back to their plan for an escape by sea.

The Spaniards took over Aminoya, near the river. They raided the village's stored corn. They began to construct boats. Suddenly, the skilled craftsmen were the important people. The carpenters, ironsmiths, caulkers, and laborers with strong backs could save them. They finished seven makeshift boats, similar to brigantines. The hogs and some of the horses were slaughtered to provide meat for the journey.

A caulker is one skilled at forcing material into cracks or joints to keep water out of a boat. In this case, the caulkers used strips of old Indian shawls.

As they worked on the boats, local Indians came begging for food. They were thin and weak; the army had taken all their winter supplies. For once, the Spaniards showed mercy. They returned some food to the Indians.

Most of the slaves (now numbering more than 500) had to be left behind. There would not be enough food and water for the Spaniards plus all of them. Many had been captured at the beginning of the entrada. They were now far from their homes and fearful of being left at the mercy of local Indians.

On July 2, 1543, more than 300 Spaniards boarded the boats. The remaining horses were loaded into pairs of canoes tied together. The horses' front feet went in one canoe and their back feet in another. The canoes were anchored to the back of the boats. They headed down the river, hoping the danger was over. It wasn't.

By the next day, Indians were in pursuit in large dugout canoes. The chronicles differ in their estimates, but there were somewhere between 50 and 100 canoes. The Indians kept up a constant flurry of arrows. Some Spaniards were killed and others wounded. The survivors were overjoyed when at last, the Indians gave up the chase.

But the boats soon sailed into the territory of another tribe determined to attack. The men quickly went ashore and slaughtered most of the remaining horses. This provided needed food and lightened the boats. Several horses were turned loose.

The Indian attacks continued, but with less ferocity as the boats neared the Gulf. They had to decide if they should risk the open sea in their flimsy boats or take the longer route to Mexico. They played it safe. The boats followed the coastline, staying in sight of shore. Clouds of mosquitoes were thick in the air. Sometimes the sails were black with them. The men had welts and were bloody from slapping the insects.

On September 11, 1543, they reached the Spanish seaport of Pánuco, Mexico. Stepping ashore, the weary men went first to the local church. They prayed and gave thanks for making it safely back to Spanish ground. The mayor sent a message to Mexico City that the survivors of the De Soto expedition had arrived. This information reached Cuba in October. Isabel de Bobadilla was now a widow. The riches she and De Soto had were gone. She soon sold her property in Cuba and returned to Spain.

In his disappointment over not finding treasure, De Soto never realized his true accomplishments in La Florida. Neither did he realize the amount of destruction his expedition had left behind. If he had known, he probably would not have cared.
De Soto and his men were the first Europeans to explore the southeastern part of the North American continent. The expedition traveled more than 2,000 miles through land that is now part of Florida, Georgia, South Carolina, North Carolina, Tennessee, Alabama, Mississippi, Arkansas, and Texas.

De Soto's treasure turned out to be knowledge. This new land—rich and diverse—would later be settled by the Spanish, French, and English. Because of the accounts kept of the expedition, important information was recorded. Reports carried back to Spain described the regions through which they traveled. They told about the appearance, cultures, and habits of sixteenth-century Native Americans.

Tales of the new land encouraged further exploration and development. Twenty-two years later, in September 1565, Pedro Menendez de Aviles founded the Spanish settlement of St. Augustine (Florida), the oldest continuously occupied city in North America.

While he is credited with the discovery of the Mississippi River, De Soto was not actually the first European to see it. Another Spaniard had explored around the mouth of the river twenty-two years before. Later in 1528, survivors of the failed Narváez expedition saw the mouth of the great river. But De Soto was the first European to explore its inland shores and the first to cross it.

The De Soto expedition brought disaster to North America's native peoples. They were killed in battle. They were worked to death as slaves. They were displaced from their homes. Thousands died of diseases brought by the Spaniards, to which they had no resistance. In wiping out so many native populations, De Soto destroyed religious, cultural, and governing traditions. How could Indians continue to believe in leaders so easily overthrown? How could they worship gods who did not protect them?

Despite their losses, the Indians frequently proved a challenge to the Spaniards. As the expedition fled down

the Mississippi ahead of attacking warriors, one native
stood in his canoe and shouted:

> *Thieves, vagabonds, and loiterers who without*
> *honor or shame travel along this coast, disquieting*
> *its inhabitants, depart this place immediately…. If*
> *we possessed such large canoes as yours…we would*
> *follow you to your own land and conquer it, for we*
> *too are men like yourselves.*

Fray Sebastián de Cañete, writing of the expedition,
compared the native cultures to that of Spain: "There is in
everything much justice and reason, as in Spain…." He and
a few others came to view the natives simply as people like
themselves. They saw the same capacity for nobility,
integrity, courage, and intelligence that were held as ideals
by European societies. De Soto, during his lifetime, did not
come to this understanding.

The explorer failed in his stated mission: to find gold, to
establish Spanish settlements, and to spread Christianity. But
throughout his travels into unknown and often hostile
country, De Soto showed the traits for which he was known
and respected—the curiosity of the true explorer, courage in
the face of danger, persistence, and the willingness to go on
in spite of huge (and often frightening) obstacles in his path.

Spanish conquistador Hernando De Soto still cannot be
ignored.

Glossary

adelantado–civil and military governor.

archaeology–the study of past humans and cultures as revealed by bones, fossils, and artifacts.

artifact–object made or used by humans, especially those from earlier times.

arquebus–portable, heavy matchlock gun.

brigantine–light, swift boat equipped for rowing and sailing.

buffer zone–neutral, unoccupied area between rival powers.

cacique–Caribbean word for "chief"; the leader of a Native American tribe or province.

caravel–light sailing ship.

cavalry–soldiers who fight on horseback.

chain mail–flexible armor made of interlocked metal rings.

chiefdom–province of Native Americans ruled by one leader

chivalry–the knight's code that includes kindness, gallantry, and courtesy to others.

chronicle–written account, diary, or journal.

civilization–society with established social, political, and cultural systems.

colony–settlement in a new territory ruled by the home country.

conquistador–conqueror; Spanish soldiers who led conquests in the Americas.

continent–large land mass such as North America, Europe, or Asia.

crossbow–weapon with a bow attached to a wooden stock; the bowstring is drawn back by a crank.

dowry–goods or money that a bride brings to her marriage.

entrada–entrance into unexplored country.

expedition–journey undertaken by a group, usually to explore or claim new land.

factor–agent; a person who does business on behalf of another.

halberd–weapon consisting of a battle ax and pike mounted on a long handle.

hardtack–hard, dry bread baked without salt that doesn't easily spoil.

heathen–unbeliever; a pagan.

hidalgo–low-ranking Spanish nobleman; a gentleman squire.

interpreter–one who translates languages or explains meanings.

isthmus–narrow strip of land connecting two larger land areas.

La Florida–Spanish name for the region that now makes up the southeastern United States.

page–young man in training to become a knight.

palisade–wall made of wooden stakes or posts.

peninsula–long, narrow portion of land that extends out into the water.

plague–fast-spreading disease that causes many deaths.

porter–one who carries a load or burden.

ransom–money or goods paid to buy the freedom of a captive.

requerimiento–statement the king of Spain required the explorers to read to natives that said they must accept Christianity or they would be killed or enslaved.

Pronunciation Guides

SPANIARDS AND OTHER EUROPEANS

Añasco (ah NYAH skoh), Juan de
Ayllón (ah YON), Lucas Vásquez de
Biedma (bee EHTH mah), Luis Hernández de
Bobadilla (boh bah THEE yah), Isabel de
Cañete (kah NYEH teh), Sebastián
De Soto (dee SOH toh), Hernando
Dürer (DEW reh), Albrecht
Elvas (EHL vas)
Gallegos (gah YEH gohs), Baltasar de
Luna y Arellano (LOO nah ee ah reh YAH no), Tristán de
Moscoso (moh SKOH soh), Luis de
Narváez (nahr VAH eth), Pánfilo de
Ortiz (ohr TEETH), Juan
Pedrarias (peth RAH ryas)
Pizarro (pee THAH roh), Francisco
Ponce de León (POHN theh theh leh OHN)
Rángel (RAHN hehl), Rodrigo
Vega (BEH gah), Garcilaso de la

INDIAN NAMES AND PLACES

Aminoya (ah mee NOY ah)
Anhaica (ahn hai EE ka)
Anilco (ah NEEL ko)
Apafalaya (ah pah fa LIE yo)
Apalachee (ah pah LATCH ee)
Aquijo (ah KEY no)

Achuse (ah CHU say)
Atahachi (ah tah HATCH ee)
Atahualpa (ah tah WAHL pah)
Casqui (KAH ski)
Cayas (KAY as)
Chiaha (chee AH ha)
Chicaza (chi KAH sa)
Cofitachequi (ke fee ta CHE ki)
Coligua (ko LEE gwa)
Coosa (KOO sa)
Coste (KOH ste)
Guachoya (gwa CHO ya)
Itaba (ee TAH ba)
Mabila (ma BEE la)
Mocozo (mo KOW zo)
Napituca (na pi TOO kah)
Ocale (oh KAH lay)
Ozita (oh zee ta)
Pacaha (pa KAH ha)
Piachi (pee AH chee)
Quigualtam (key GWAL tam)
Quiguate (key GWAH the)
Talisi (TAH lee see)
Tascaluza (tahs ka LOO sah)
Tula (TOO la)
Uribahali (oo ree ba HAH lee)
Urriparacoxi (oo ree pa rah KOSH ee)
Utiangue (oo tee AHN gay)
Uxapita (oo sha PEE ta)

Further Reading

Carson, Robert. *The World's Great Explorers: Hernando De Soto*. Chicago: Children's Press, 1991.

Gallagher, Jim. *Hernando de Soto and the Exploration of Florida*. Philadelphia: Chelsea House Publishers, 2000.

Whitman, Sylvia. *Hernando de Soto and the Explorers of the American South*. New York and Philadelphia: Chelsea House Publishers, 1991.

About the Author

Faye Gibbons is the author of ten children's books, including *Mountain Wedding* (Child Study Children's Book Committee Book of the Year), *King Shoes and Clown Pockets* (*USA Today* list of Best Books for Kids 1989), *Night in the Barn* (PBS Storytime title), and *Mighty Close to Heaven* (American Library Association Best Book List). Her essays and children's stories have appeared in *Old House Journal* and *Highlights for Children*. She lives in Deatsville, Alabama.

Index